WELSH

PLACE NAMES

Conwy Castle

JOHN JONES

WELSH PLACE NAMES

first published by John Jones Cardiff Ltd., June 1979
New edition © JOHN JONES (PUBLISHING) LTD., 1983
New edition, with additional text and new cover, March 1996

ISBN 1 871083 10 9

Geoff's Trains
69 Pitt Street
Kidderminster
DY10 2UN
England
www.geoffs-trains.com

Illustrations by Maldwyn Roberts
Illustrations of Aberdyfi, p10, by Eric Jones

Cover design by Design Principle, Cardiff

Printed by CPD Wales, Ebbw Vale

Published by
JOHN JONES (PUBLISHING) LTD.
Reg. Office:
Barclays Bank Chambers,
St. Peter's Square,
Ruthin, Denbighshire

INTRODUCTION

To write a book on the meaning of place names in any language is to lay oneself open to criticism from all sides. So many of our present-day names bear little resemblance to their original forms because of corruptions, mutations and errors, that it is far too easy to make a mistake, however innocently. Names that appear to be easily explained on first glance turn out to have completely different meanings after deeper research. Take as an example the name of LICHFIELD near Birmingham. Superficially it would seem that it derives from LICH, the Middle English word for a corpse, and FIELD: a field where once there was a corpse or corpses. The correct definition, however, is that the name comes from the old British (Celtic) word LEITOCAITON, which became shortened to LICCED, and FELD being added to it. LEIT meant grey; CAIT was wood, so that the name really means the field of the grey wood. The Roman form was LETOCETUM and the Welsh name for Lichfield is still CAERLWYTGOED (town or fort of the grey wood). Similarly the names of some places in Wales are of English origin, such as GWESPYR (originally Westbury) or BISTRE (originally Bishopstree).

Local dialects have played a large part in disguising the original form of a name, as have sloppy pronounciations for the sake of ease and convenience. Many changes can also be attributed to mistakes made by scribes copying from older documents. Nevertheless it is possible to work out the meanings of many place names, especially if a few key words such as ABER, LLAN and BETWS are explained.

ABER is derived from AD-BER or OD-BER, meaning where two waters meet, either two rivers or a river flowing into the sea. It is usually followed by the name of the river. Very many river names end in -WY, which can lend to some confusion and the mistaken idea that WY was the old Welsh word for water. In fact it derives from one of two words. In some cases it comes from DWYW, or DWYWES, meaning a goddess (all rivers being feminine). One example of this is the DYFRDWY (Dee), meaning the waters of the goddess, or holy waters. Similarly two rivers in Gwynedd are called DWYFOR and DWYFACH, the large (Dwyfor) and the small (Dwyfach) river goddesses. They flow together at LLANYSTUMDWY, which means where the two rivers twist and meet together. Dover in England derives from the same source.

The other derivation of WY comes from GWY, meaning turnings or meanderings. The river Wye, GWY in Welsh, simply means the river with many turnings. The river TAWE was originally TAWY and meant the quiet (from TAWEL) and twisting (from GWY) water. Very many rivers were dedicated to pre-Christian deities, and their names survive to this day, as with ABERAERON deriving from AERON the goddess of war, and ABERDARON, from DARON the goddess of the oak trees.

It is interesting that many rivers in Wales refer to pigs in their names, either TWRCH (boar), BANW or HWCH (sow). OGWEN comes from this source, the original name being OGFANW. OG comes from AWG meaning fast, sharp, and BANW is a sow. BANFF in Scotland is of the same derivation. Could this be that there was some god or goddess who took the form of a pig, or does it refer to the way the water forces its way through the land, like a pig routing with its snout? Or could they all be references to the tales of the MABINOGI, a collection of Welsh legends, where pigs often played a leading part? In the story of CULHWCH AND OLWEN, Culhwch (note the form HWCH at the end of his name, from when he was found being suckled by a wild sow) in order to win the hand of Olwen, had to perform three tasks, one of which was to capture the TWRCH TRWYTH, a wild boar, and retrieve a golden comb from the hair between its ears. In another tale, that of MATH SON OF MATHONWY, Prince of Gwynedd, Math coveted a special herd of pigs that had been given to PRYDERI Prince of Dyfed by ARAWN the King of ANNWN (which was Hell). The pigs were driven from the south to the north, and places bearing the names MOCH, TWRCH or BANW were said to be some of their resting places, e.g. *MOCH*DRE, NANT Y *MOCH*, LLANRHAEADR-YM-*MOCH*NANT.

CYMER is also a name for where waters meet. It derives from COM (together) and BÊR, a common old name for water. CYMERAU is the plural form, as in RHYDCYMERAU, the ford where two rivers join. QUIMPER in Britanny has the same meaning, as has INVER in Scotland. BLAEN means the head of the river, BLAENAU being the plural form as in BLAENAU FFESTINIOG. PISTYLL means a cataract and RHAEADR means a waterfall, although in South Wales these features are sometimes referred to as SGWD or YSGWD. CLAIS or GLAIS means a ditch. LLWCH can mean a lake, but it may also be a marsh or a mire. It has the same derivation as LOCH in Scotland and LOUGH in Ireland. LLWCHWR means muddy water, and AMLWCH means beside the marsh.

Places named after rivers and lakes form only a small part of Welsh etymology. Very many places are called after other geographical features such as hills, mountains and valleys. DYFFRYN (valley) comes from DWFR (water) and HYNT (course or path). It started off meaning the river bed only but by now the word means the whole valley. NANT means the course of the river or a stream, similar to the modern meaning of DYFFRYN. It is often shortened to NAN at the beginning of a name, as in NANMOR (NANT + MAWR) meaning a large nant. NANHORON would originally have been NANT HORON. Very often NANT is followed by the name of a person, as in NANT FFRANCON. FFRANCON comes from FFRANC, a recorded ninth century word for a mercenary soldier. These mercenaries would probably have been of the Teutonic peoples who also gave their name to France. NANT GWRTHEYRN is another example. Gwrtheyrn being Voritgern, a sixth century ruler, who supposedly first hired Angles and Saxons as mercenaries and gave them lands on the eastern shores of Britain. He was overthrown by Ambrosius, brother of Uther Pendragon who was said to be the father of King Arthur.

CWM means a dish shaped hollow, or small hanging valley. KOMM means a dish in the Gaelic, and KOMBANT is found in Brittany meaning a valley. In Greek the word for a cup or bowl is KUMBE, so at one time the word must have been fairly common all over Europe. It is the same word as COMBE in English, as in ILFRACOMBE. PANT also means a small hollow. YSTRAD has often been taken to derive from the Latin STRATA, but this is not so. Both words were derived form an older language, the Welsh coming from the BRYTHONEG, and both have a similar meaning. It means a flat area of land, such as the bottom of a valley. It is often accompanied by the name of a river, such as YSTRAD GYNLAIS, or by the name of the person who at one time owned the land. DOL means a meadow and can also mean the oxbows formed by a very old river in its meanderings, as in DOLAU COTHI, the meanderings of the river COTHI. YNYS means an island, but this name is often found on places inland. Probably it signified dry land surrounded by a river or marsh. It is similar to INIS in Ireland, or HOLM in English. Over the years the word YNYS in some instances became shortened to a single S as in SKETTY in Swansea (from YNYS GETTI) or SKENFRITH in Gwent (YNYS GYNWRAIDD).

MAES is a field. It can be found in its complete form as in MAESYFED, or it can found as MA at the beginning of a word or ·FA at the end of a word. MACHYNLLETH means the field of Cynllaith, and CYFARTHFA means the place where hounds barked ferociously, probably holding its quarry at bay. GWENT can also mean a field. It is found in words such as MYNWENT (cemetery).

MOEL can mean bald or barren, or it can mean a hill. Possibly it meant a barren hill top. MOELFRE in Anglesey comes from MOEL meaning barren and BRE meaning hill. DRWS is usually found to mean a gateway or pass. BWLCH has the same meaning. DRWS Y COED means pass of the trees, DRWS Y NANT means gateway to the valley, and BWLCH YR OERDDRWS means the pass of the cold gateway (in fact it is situated high up in the mountains above Dolgellau, a cold and bleak place). ALLT in North Wales means a hill, but in South Wales it means a wooded slope. LLANFAIRYMUALLT (the Welsh name for Builth Wells) means the church of St. Mary by the wooded slope with cattle on it. ARDD means high land,

and has the same base as ARD in Scotland and Ireland. ERDDIG means a small hill, a little ARDD. BAN means the top of a mountain or a high place. It originally meant a cow's horn, and any mountain named BAN would presumably be horn shaped.

Many places also have the names of plants or animals incorporated in them. Perhaps one of the most common is Y GELLI, the Welsh for a grove of trees. This word can be found in many place names such as GELLIFOR (the large grove), GELLIDAWEL (the quiet grove) and even GELLI DOCHLAETHE (the grove of ghosts or apparitions!). PRYS can also mean a grove, as can LLWYN. HALKYN stems from HELYGAIN, a grove of willow trees. BEDWAS means a grove of birch trees. DERLWYN means a grove of oak trees. CLYNNOG stems from CELYNNAWG, a place full of holly; EITHINOG from a place full of gorse; MAWNOG from a place where peat is found, and RHEDYNOG from a place full of bracken.

CRAF was an old word for garlic, and can be found in places like ABERCRAF and CRAFNANT. Presumably the first means the river where garlic grows, the second the valley where garlic grows. ALAW means a water lily: LLYN ALAW means the lake of the water lilies. AFAN means rasberries – they must have been growing profusely on the banks of a river for it to be called AFAN as in ABERAFAN. EFROG, the Welsh name for YORK, comes form EFWR which means cow parsnip.

An interesting name, and one very difficult to define, is BETWS. It is very common throughout Wales, often followed by the name of a person, or a description. At one time it was assumed that all the BETWS referred to churches or religious establishments. However in north east Wales BETWS very clearly refers to a wooded slope of birch trees. This then would be derived from the old Welsh word BETGUOS, the same base as the name BEDWAS above. Probably differences in dialect and pronunciation led BETGUOS to become BEDWAS in one area and BETWS in another. The most popular derivation of the ecclesiastical BETWS is from the Old English BED-HUS and Middle English BEDE HUS, or bead house. BEAD means prayer, and HUS means house. From the study of each parish where there is a BETWS, it would appear that a BETWS is where there is a church secondary to the main parish church. The Oxford Dictionary defines a Beadhouse as 'a house of prayer, hence an alms-house, in which prayers are to be offered for the soul of the founder'. This definition might help explain the fact that there are no places in England named after a beadhouse as there are in Wales. The Welsh BETWS has kept that original English meaning of a house of prayer, which would correspond to an oratory in modern English, whereas in modern times a beadhouse would mean an almshouse.

As one travels through Wales one can see how great an influence religion had on the names of communities. By far the most common prefix is LLAN. Originally this word meant an enclosed piece of land. It is still used as a suffix to denote various types of store areas, for example GWINLLAN (vineyard); PERLLAN (orchard) and YDLAN (granary) corresponding to the English YARD. In time it came to mean a piece of land dedicated by or to a saint, many of whom lived during the sixth and seventh centuries. Within its bounds would be built a cell, or CELL, as in DOLGELLAU, the meadow of the cells. The occupant of a cell would gather disciples and so eventually form a church, then possibly a monastery would be established.

A LLAN is usually followed by the name of the saint to whom the church is dedicated. Sometimes it is followed by the number of saints commemorated by the church, as in LLANDDEUSANT (two saints), LLANPUMSAINT (five saints) and even LLANDEUDDEGSAINT (twelve saints!). Very many of these saints, both male and female, would have belonged to the Celtic Church, which came to be regarded as heretical by Rome. Germanicus, a Bishop in France, was sent to Britain by Rome to crush the heretics, which he did quite ruthlessly. Evidence of his travels can be found in the number of LLANARMONs (GARMON being the Welsh form of his name) that are scattered throughout Wales.

Many other saints have more than one church dedicated to them all over Wales. All the LLANGYBIs are dedicated to St. CYBI, who supposedly spent a great part of his life at CAERGYBI (Holyhead) on the north west coast of Anglesey. There is a legend that St. Cybi used to journey every day from Holyhead to the centre of Anglesey, there to meet a fellow saint, St. Seiriol. Seiriol came from Ynys Seiriol, now popularly known as Puffin Island, off the south east coast of Anglesey. They discussed theology for some hours, then each would travel back to his own cell. St. Cybi walked eastwards every morning and westwards every evening, so always facing the sun, whilst St. Seiriol walked westwards in the mornings and eastwards in the evenings, so always having his back to the sun. Now they are commonly known as SEIRIOL WYN A CHYBI FELYN (white Seiriol and yellow Cybi).

St. David, the patron saint of Wales, also has a number of churches dedicated to him. His monastery was situated at St. David's in Pembroke, and is now the smallest cathedral city in Britain, having a large cathedral in a tiny village. St. David was a DYFRWR, that is of a religious order that forbade the drinking of anything except water (DYFRWYR meaning water man). More evidence of this order can be found at LLANDDOWROR, which is a corruption of LLANDDYFRWR.

A LLAN can also be followed by a description of its situation, as in LLANGOED, the llan by the wood, or LLANLLYFNI, the llan by the river LLYFNI (meaning still waters). LLANDRE might be mistaken for LLAN and TREF, the church by the town, but in fact it comes from LLODRE,

7

deriving from LLAWD + RE, similar to the Gaelic LATHRACH, meaning the site of a house or church. In modern Welsh LLODRE has come to mean trousers from its original from LLODRAU.

Other religious establishments are recorded in place names such as DYSERTH, which stems from the Latin DESERTUM, and was a retreat for a hermit. TY was used to demote the main monastery of a saint, as in the Welsh for St. David's, TY DDEWI. MYNACHDY (MYNACH means monk, DY is from TY, a house) would in fact mean a farmhouse belonging to a monastery. MERTHYR in modern Welsh means a martyr, but when it is used in a place name together with the name of a saint, as in MERTHYR TYDFIL, it denotes the place where the saint was either killed or buried.

Men have left their mark on place names not only through religious establishments but also through places of war. Perhaps the most common of this type is CAER, meaning an enclosed, fortified place. Some say it comes form the Latin CASTRA whilst others, possibly more correctly, say it comes from the same stem as CAU, to close, shut or bar. Examples of CAER are plentiful, as in CAERNARFON, the CAER in ARFON, CAERDYDD (Cardiff) the CAER on the river TAFF. Many Welsh name forms for English place names contain the prefix CAER, as in CAERLOYW (Gloucester); CAERLIWELYDD (Carlisle); CAERGAINT (Canterbury); CAERGRAWNT (Cambridge) etc.

Another type of fortified place was DINAS, or DIN. Today this word would mean city, but it derives from the Celtic form DOUNON which was Latinised to DUNUM in place names on the continent. DIN corresponds to TUN in Old English, which gives -TON in so many English place names. It meant a safe place to stay in. DINBYCH (Denbigh) means a small DIN, whilst DINMOR means a large one.

PENTREF today means a village, but in olden times it would mean the place where the lord's serfs lived. They were bound to the land and if the lord sold the land they would be sold with it. Thus PENTREFELIN would be where the serfs worked a mill (MELIN meaning a mill).

The list of place names that describe people's names or occupations would be endless. A dictionary might be useful in finding out the meaning of many parts of words. In this book an attempt has been made to define the meaning of some places of interest in Wales, but the list here is only a very small part of all the names that exist. It is a fascinating study which can throw light on the way of life of our ancestors over a thousand years ago. It is hoped that this little booklet will help the visitor to Wales understand some of its rich and varied history by describing in historical terms some of the place names of Wales. It is by no means exhaustive, and in some cases the reader is left to decide for himself what a name might mean. It's all part of the fun and interest!

THE PRONUNCIATION OF WELSH

Speaking Welsh is similar in sound to speaking Spanish or Russian. The sound are made positively and with vigour; some by blowing outwards. The **ch** is made by compressing air through the back of the throat (exactly as in the Scottish **loch**). The **ll** is made by placing the tip of the tongue against the front top of the mouth and blowing air beneath it through one side. Many Welsh place names begin with **Llan,** so listen to how Welsh speakers say it and copy them. Do not hesitate to ask Welsh speakers to help you with pronunciation; they will be pleased.

The Welsh alphabet is as follows: A B C CH D DD E F FF G NG H I J L LL M N O P PH R RH S T TH U W Y. Pronunciations are generally phonetic, so when the sounds of the above are mastered, you simply put them together in word order to pronounce the word. The following is a general guide. **Consonants.** b,d,h,j,l,m,n,p,s,t are sounded as in English. But the following are distinct. **c** is hard, as in 'cat'. **ch,** a distinct Welsh sound, see above. **dd,** tip of tongue against top teeth, as in 'them'. **f,** soft, as in 'vessel'. **ff,** bottom lip against top teeth, as in 'funnel'. **g,** as in 'go'. **ng,** as in 'bring'. **ll,** see above – and practise! **r,** a vigorous sound as in 'ringing'. **rh,** the **r** followed by a chesty outward bow which is the **h,** as in 'who'. **th** as in 'thick'. **Vowels a,** the sound of a sheep baaaing. **e;** watch this one, it isn't the English e as in 'eating', it's the sound you make when you haven't quite heard someone, 'eh . . .eh . . .'. **i** as in 'Ee bah gum', or 'bee'. **o** as in middle of 'call'. **w** as in 'coo'. **u,** here the mouth is made into a funnel at the front, and there is no English equivalent. **y,** as in 'up'.

Mutation is a feature of Welsh. This is the process where the basic word given in a dictionary is changed in writing or speaking. The change applies to an initial consonant or of a vowel in the first syllable. The reason for such changes is buried deep in the spoken habits of Welsh-speakers. Generally mutations occur in order to make the sounds easier to say and facilitate word-sound flow. 'Craig' (rock) can be changed to 'graig'; 'pel' to 'bel' (ball) and 'gwers' (lesson) to 'ngwers'.

Don't be afraid of saying it badly! The best way of learning how to pronounce a language is to listen to it spoken in a native context and copy the sounds. Keep listening. Say it. Keep trying!

Aberdyfi

A

ABBEY CWM HIR. *Cwm Hir* means a long narrow valley. A Cistercian abbey was founded here in 1143 by Cadwallon ab Madog which was later destroyed by Owain Glyn Dŵr in the 15th century.

ABER. The mouth of a river or stream usually where it joins the sea.

ABERAERON. Situated at the mouth of the Aeron. *Aer* meant a battle, and the river was dedicated to the goddess of battle.

ABERAFAN. The mouth of the river Afan. *Afan* was an old Welsh name for raspberries, or it could have been derived from *-ban*, meaning height, or from *llafan*, a kind of seaweed.

ABERCRAF. The confluence of the river Craf with the Tawe. *Craf* was the old word for garlic and many river banks abound with this pungent-smelling plant. Alternatively it could derive from *crafu*, to claw, and this could describe the way the river has carved out its channel.

ABERDÂR. The name of the river Dâr could derive from the number of oak trees *(dar,* or *derw)* growing along its banks, or it could be a shortened form of *dyar*, meaning noisy water.

ABERDARON. A village situated at the mouth of the river Daron, *Daron* being a name anciently applied to the goddess of the oak. This picturesque fishing village was the birthplace of Richard Robert Jones, alias *Dic Aberdaron*, born in 1778. He was a famous, if eccentric, linguist and it is said he was conversant with thirteen languages. He was always surrounded by cats!

ABERDYFI. A village situated on the mouth of the river Dyfi. The name could derive from a number of different sources. It could come *from Dof-wy*, the smooth or tame water, or from *Dyfn-wy*, the deep or dark water, stemming from the Gaelic *'dheubh'*, black.

ABERFAN. The river Fan, meaning a high place, joins the Taff at this village, scene of the great tragedy of 1966, when the village school was buried by a collapsing coal tip.

ABERFFRAW. The village situated at the mouth of the river Ffraw. *Ffraw* means agitation, flooding. In Roman times it was known as Gadavia. Later it was one of the three Royal residences of Wales and the seat of the chief courts of justice. *Ffraw* has the same meaning as *frome* in Hereford and Dorset.

ABERGAVENNY. In Welsh it is known as *Y Fenni* or *Abergyfenni. Gyfenni* derives from *Gobannion, Gofannon* in the Mabinogi, a blacksmith.

ABERGELE. A village situated at the mouth of the river Gele, originally *Gelau*, which means a blade or sword, describing the course of the river.

ABERGLASLYN. The mouth of the river Glaslyn, meaning blue water or blue lake. Today Aberglaslyn is in fact situated some miles inland, but before Maddocks built the cob at Porthmadog the sea came up as far as Aberglaslyn, Nantmor and Llanfrothen.

ABERGWESYN. Here the river Gwesyn and Irfon join. *Gwesyn* is an old Welsh word for a shepherd. In this case he was said to be the shepherd of Goronwy ab Ednyfain. The district was noted for its sheep rearing.

ABERGWILI. A village situated at the mouth of the river Gwili. *Gwili* is derived from *gwyllt*, wild, and *lli*, flow of water.

ABERHAFESP. The river Hafesp and Severn join at this point. *Hafesp* means a river which runs dry in summer.

ABERMULE. The river Mule joins the Severn here. Mule is probably a corruption of *mudliw*, meaning a river that changes its colour. The English motley is derived from the same word.

ABERPORTH. The mouth of the river forms a natural harbour here, hence the name – mouth of the harbour.

ABERSOCH. A village situated at the mouth of the river Soch, which means a sink, drain or ditch. The river is generally rather muddy.

ABERSYCHAN. The mouth of the river Sychan, meaning the river which runs dry in summer.

ABERYSTWYTH. Situated at the confluence of the Ystwyth and Rheidiol where they meet the sea. *Ystwyth* means smooth water. Before the reign of Queen Elizabeth I it was known as Llanbadarn Gaerog, meaning the fortified church of St. Padarn.

AFON. River.

ALLT. Hillside, Steep road, Cliff, A wood.

AMBLESTON. The town of Hamill, a Viking who founded a colony there.

AMLWCH. This may be derived from *am*, around, and *llwch*, muddy water, lake or mouth. It is akin to the Irish *lough* and *Scottish loch*.

AMMANFORD. The Welsh form is *Rhydaman*, the ford over the river Aman. There is reference in the Mabinogi to King Arthur and his men hunting the *Twrch Trwyth*, – a boar, and killing one of his sows by the Amanw. The river was dedicated to the goddess Amanwy.

AMROTH. *Am* – means to encircle, whilst – *roth* could stem from the Gaelic *ráth*, a mound or fortified town, or from the old Welsh *rhath*, to claw, to file, which would describe the flow of the river Rath which runs nearby.

BACH. Small. Can be a term of endearment. An older meaning refers to a nook or corner.

BAGILLT. This name probably derives from the English Backelie, as it appears in 1086. The word was changed to Backelegh in 1325 and Bagild in 1539. It means Bacga's lea or meadow.

BAGLAN. An abbreviation of Llanfaglan, the church of St. Baglan, a 6th century Welsh saint.

BALA. This name could derive from the Celtic for village, or from the word *ball* – to shoot forth. Thus *Bala coed*, trees in bud, and *Bala llyn*, the outlet of the lake – Llyn Tegid.

BANC. A mound or small hill.

BANGOR. The derivation of the name for this city is problematical but is most likely derived from *ban*, meaning a bond or strengthening, and *cor*, meaning woven. Thus a protective hedge was woven to enclose a settlement or church. Eventually the enclosed land rather than its protection gained the name.

BANGOR IS COED. A sanctuary, probably fortified, situated below the wood. It is the site of an ancient monastery founded prior to 180 A.D. by the son of Coel, the first Christian king of Britain.

BARGOED. The full name is *Pont Aber Bargoed*, the bridge over the Bargoed where it joins the river Rhymney. *Bargoed* derives from *Bargawd* or *Bargodion*, a name given to the Welsh marches or boundaries; it means edge or rim.

BARMOUTH. An Anglicised form of *Abermaw, bar* being a mutation of *aber*, the mouth of the river Maw. *Maw* means broad, whilst *Mawddach* (the actual name of the river) means overflowing water. The English form came into use in the 18th century when shipowners demanded an English name as the home port of their vessels.

BARRY. The island used to belong to Gerald de Barry and his family, one of whom was an inquisitor in the survey of the Lordship of Glamorgan in 1262. The family also gave their name to the town on the mainland.

BASALEG. This is not a corruption of *Maesaleg* (Alex's Field) as was once supposed. but a borrowing from the Latin and Greek word for church – *basilica*.

BEAUMARIS. The Welsh origins of the name of this town is obscure. There are many Welsh versions, the chief being *Biwmares*. In ancient times

13

The Church at Beaumaris

it was called *Porth Wygyr* – a port by the fresh wood. Its present name was given to the town by Edward I when the castle was built in 1285. The most popular derivation of the name is from the French *beau*, beautiful, and *maree*, sea – place by the beautiful sea. Or *beau marais* – a place by the beautiful marsh.

BEDD. Grave.

BEDDGELERT. This means Gelert's or Celert's grave. The most popular interpretation of this name (suspected to date from a 19th century entrepreneur) is the legend of Prince Llewelyn and his faithful hound Gelert. The prince went hunting one day and left the dog to guard his baby son. When he returned he found the cradle overturned and the dog's jaws stained with blood. In a rage he slew the hound, then heard his baby crying under the cradle. In a corner he found the body of an enormous wolf. The prince had Gelert buried with honour and erected a church as a memorial to Gelert and thanks to God for the safety of his son. Less romantically the name could derive from the grave of Celert ap Math, a descendent of an Irish prince who came there in the 4th century. Or it could refer to St. Celer, the patron saint of Llangeler.

BEDWAS. From the old Welsh word *betguos*, meaning a grove of small birch trees.

BEDWELLTY. The original spelling of this name may have been *Bodfelltan*, meaning the place of a fast-flowing stream.

BEDGUILDY. Probably a corruption of *bugeil-dŷ*, the shepherd's house.

BERLLAN. Orchard.

BERRIEW. This is a corruption of *Aber-rhiw*, where the river Rhiw joins the river Severn. *Rhiw* means a slope.

BERTH. A hedge or wood.

BERWYN. Mountain covered in snow (*gwyn*-white).

BETHESDA. The original name of this village was *Cilfoden*. Its present name derives from the Congregational chapel built there in 1819.

BETWS GARMON. *Betws* in this instance means a religious house, dedicated to St. Garmon. St. Garmon's well can be found about a mile distant.

BETWS GWERFYL GOCH. Prayer house of Gwerfyl the Red.

BETWS Y COED. *Betws*, in this sense, is derived from *bedwas*, the plural of *bedw*, a birch grove. In North-east Wales the word was used to signify a steep slope covered by birch trees. Similarly *betws* can be found in old manuscripts describing terrain over-run by bushes and small trees. So in this case we have a birch wood on hilly slopes.

BLAEN. The front end. Top edge. Head of a valley.

BLAENAFON. This is a combination of *blaen*, the head of a valley, and *afon*, river. Thus, a river at the head of the valley.

BLAENAU. This name is the plural of *blaen*, which means the head of a valley or source of a river. At this point the heads of the valleys meet.

BLAENAU FFESTINIOG. The heads of the valleys (*blaenau*) in the land belonging to Ffestin.

BODEDERN. *Bod* – a dwelling place. *Edern*, or *Ederyn*, was the son of Nudd, the son of Seli. Edeyrn was a fierce warrior and a poet, and by the end of his life a religious man. He built a church here, which was later dedicated to him.

BODFFORDD. A compound of *bod*, a dwelling, and *ffordd*, a road or track.

BODFARI. *Bod* – dwelling place; *fari* derives from *Varis*, a Roman station situated in the area.

BONT. A bridge.

BONVILSTON. Both the English and the Welsh name, *Tresimwn*, derive from Simon Bonville, chief steward of Sir Robert Fitzhamon. Many Normans gave their own names to villages in Glamorgan simply because they couldn't pronounce the Welsh.

BORTH. Harbour or bay. Entrance.

BORTH Y GEST. From *Porth* – port, *y* – the, and *gest* from *cêst*, meaning belly, abdomen, or paunch. The mountain behind is similarly called *Moel y Gêst*.

BOUGHROOD. This could be a corruption of *buwch-ffrwd*, the cow's stream, or it could derive from *bach-rhyd*, the little ford, crossing the river Wye.

BRAWDY. From the ancient Welsh word *brawd*, meaning judgement. *Dŷ* means house. There was probably a court of law near here at one time.

BRECON. The Welsh name is *Aberhonddu*, originally *Aber Hodni*, meaning the calm, black water. The river Honddu joins the Usk at this point. The English name was used after 1606, being an anglicised form of the name *Brychan*, who ruled the area around 400 A.D. and gave his name to both the town and the county.

BRIDGEND. The Welsh name is *Penybont-ar-Ogwr*, the bridge end on the river Ogmore. *Ogwr* derives from *Og-*, meaning sharp, fast, and *dŵr*, water. The fast flowing river.

BRITON FERRY. A 16th century Welsh name was *Llan-is-awel*, the sheltered church, or *Llansawel*, from the patron saint of the church, *Sawyl Benuchel*. Some say the name comes from the time when Morgan ab Caradog ab Iestyn built a tower there to prevent the Normans crossing the river on their way from Aberogwr to Cydweli.

BRONLLYS. During the Dark Ages many battles were fought in this area, and there is a strong possibility that a *llys*, or court, was held in the vicinity. *Bron* means a hillside. Thus, the court on the hill. However, the original spelling may have been *Brwynllys*, meaning the court of rushes the court of *Brwyn*.

BRYMBO. *Brym*, a corruption of *bryn*, a hill. *Bo* might probably be an abbreviation of *boda*, a kite; Red Kites are still found in Wales. More prosaically it might be derived from *baw*, meaning dirt.

BRYNAMAN. Hill of the river Aman.

BRYN SAITH MARCHOG. Between Corwen and Ruthin. Hill of the seven horsemen or Knights.

BRYNSIENCYN. *Bryn* – a hill. *Siencyn* is the Welsh form of Jenkin, which means pretty John.

BUILTH WELLS. The Welsh name is *Llanfair-ym-Muallt*, the church of St. Mary in the cow pasture. *Muallt* is a mutation of *Buallt*, a cow pasture, while Builth is an English corruption of the word.

BWLCH. Gap or pass.

BWTHYN. Small house. Cottage.

C

CAERGEILIOG. This is a compound of *caer*, a fortress, and *ceiliog*, which means cock. *Caer* is probably derived from *cau*, to shut.

CAERLEON. The present Welsh name is a corruption of *Caer y Lleng*, fort of the legion. Caerleon was the largest Roman base in Wales and as Isca Silurum was the home of the Second Augustan Legion. The most obvious feature of the Roman presence which remains still to be seen is the amphitheatre. Caerleon also has links with King Arthur as he is said to have held court at Caerleon.

CAERNARFON. From *Caer-yn-Arfon;* the fortified town in Arfon. The Romans garrisoned the town and called it Segontium. In 1282 Edward I built the castle and presented the Welsh with the first English Prince of Wales.

CAERSWS. *Caer*, the fortress, of Sws, either a personal name in itself or a contraction of *Swsan*, Susan. It may refer to a Roman station which lies nearby.

CAERWENT. This is a combination of *caer*, a fortification, and *gwent*, a plain or field – a fortress on the plain.

CAPEL CURIG. *Capel* means chapel. *Curig* was the son of Ilid, and a seventh century Welsh saint. The church is dedicated to Curig and his mother.

CAPELYFFIN. *Capel*, chapel; *y* – on or of the; *ffin*, boundary.

CARDIFF. The modern Welsh spelling is *Caerdydd*, which is a colloquial variation of *Caerdaf*, a fort on the river *Tâf* or Taff. The word has the same origins as Tam, as in Thames and Tamar, and means dark or black.

CARDIGAN (Ceredigion). The area belonging to Ceredig.

CAREW. Probably a corruption of *caerau*, wall or fortifications.

CARMARTHEN. This is a corruption of the Welsh *Caerfyrddin*, the town of *Myrddin* (Merlin). In Roman times it was known as Maridunum. Merlin was born there somtime in the fifth or sixth centuries A.D., and spent the greater part of his life in a cave near the town. A very ancient oak tree still exists in the town, known as Merlin's Oak, dating from his lifetime. It is said that as long as the oak remains, Carmarthen will not be conquered.

CARNO. From *carn*, a heap of stones or cairn. Carno is a place abounding in cairns.

CARREG CENNEN. Rock of the river Cennen.

CARROG. Fast-flowing stream.

CARTREF. Home.

CASTELL. Castle.

CASTLE MARTIN. The southern tip of Dyfed was one of the earliest Norman settlements in Wales. Castle Martin commemorates the castle built and inhabited by the family of Martin de Tours. Its older name is *Bwlch-y-clawdd*, the pass of the hillside.

CEFNLLYS. This is derived from *cefn*, a hillside or ridge, and *llys*, a court. The court may refer to the castle built here by Ralph Mortimer around the year 1242, or to much earlier constructions which were Welsh defences against the Saxon invaders.

CEINEWYDD. A compound of *cei*, quay, and *newydd*, new. New Quay.

CEMAES. Is derived from the old Welsh and Gaelic word *cammas*, which is also found in Scotland. It means a turn in the river, or a fort in the road.

CERRIG Y DRUDION. This is a compound of *cerrig*, stones or crag, and *dewrion*, valiant men or warriors. The crag of the warriors.

CERRIG Y GWYDDYL. *Cerrig*, stones; *y Gwyddyl*, of the Irishmen.

CHEPSTOW. The Welsh name is *Casgwent*, which is a compound of *cas*, a fort, and *gwent*, field.

CILCENNIN. From *cil*, a nook or source of a stream, and *cennin*, the stream itself, which may have been named after St. Cennyn.

CILCWM. A combination of *cil*, the source of a stream, and *cwm*, bowl-shaped valley.

CILMERI. The name is derived from *cil*, a nook or sheltered spot, and *meri*, from *mwyaren*, a bramble.

CLARACH. This is the name of the river, which is probably derived from *claer*, meaning bright or clear, and the Celtic suffix – *ach*, meaning water.

CLAWDD. Hedge; raised bank. A characteristic Welsh hedge of earth with turf or stones; seen in the Llyn Peninsula.

CLYDACH. This is the name of the river which means a stream with a rocky bed or sheltered stream. The suffix – *ach* is common in Welsh river names, derived from the old Celtic, meaning water. *Agh*, which in Ireland means a ford, and the Scottish – *och* have the same derivation.

CLYNNOG. This is a contraction of *celyn*, a holly tree, and *awg*, many. Clynnog, the place of many holly trees. Clynnog with its fine ancient church is located on the north coast of Lleyn, on the A499, about six miles west of Caernarfon.

COED. Trees. Wood.

COLWYN. This name could derive from the name of Bran ap Llyr Lledaith's chief shepherd, Colwyn, or it could be a compound of *cau*, enclosed hollow, and *llwyn*, a grove – the grove in the hollow.

CONWY. The town was founded by Maelgwyn Gwynedd in 581 and was then known as *Caer Gyffin*, the border town. The site of Conwy castle, built by Edward I in 1283, was known as Conovium. The present name of the town is taken from the river which derives its name either from *cawn*, reeds, or the same spelling meaning fulness – the mighty river.

CORWEN. It is most probably derived from *cor*, a high or sacred place, and *maen*, stone, its original spelling being *Corfaen*.

CRAI. The word means fresh, or raw. Some believe that, when used in a geographical sense, the word denotes a hollow in a valley.

CRICIETH. The spelling of this name has varied a great deal through the years. It could derive from *crug*, meaning heap or mound, and *aeth*, sorrow or pain. Or it could come from *crug-caeth*, the narrow hill. Then again it could be *craig-aeth*, the sorrowful rock.

CRICKHOWEL. The Welsh form is *Crughywel*, the cairn of Hywel. The Hywel referred to was prince of Glamorgan whose boundaries were defined by heaps of stones.

CROSS HANDS. Most probably named after a public house.

CROESYCEILIOG. *Croes* means a cross or crossroads; *ceiliog* means a cock or weathercock.

CRUGYBAR. *Crug*, heap of stones or cairn, *y bar*, of the peak.

CWM. A small, rounded, valley.

CWMBRAN. This is the vale of the river *Brân*, the dark river.

CWMDUAD. The valley of the river Duad. *Duad* implies darkness or blackness.

CWMGWENDRAETH. The valley of the river *Gwendraeth*, the white beach.

CWMIOY. This a corruption of *cwm*, a hollow, dish-shaped valley (the English coombe is derived from this word), and *iau*, meaning yoke. The whole probably describes the shape of the valley itself.

CWMTWRCH. A compound of *cwm*, hollow, valley, and *twrch*, boar. The boar's hollow. The river which flows through this valley is also called Twrch.

CWM RHEIDOL. The valley of the river Rheidol. *Rheidol* may be a contraction of *rhyd-y-ddôl*, the stream of the meadow.

D

DALE. This is most probably the Norse word, frequently found in English place names, which means a broad valley.

DAN. Under.

DAROWEN. Owen's oak trees, from *dâr* or its plural *derw*, meaning Oak.

DEFYNNOG. The derivation of this name is uncertain though it probably comes from a personal name. It may derive from the 6th century St. Defynog, or the correct spelling may well have been *Tref Cynog*, the home of Cynog, a 5th century saint who founded a church here.

DENBIGH. The name of this town is most probably an anglicised from *Dinbych*, from *din*, itself derived from the Celtic *dounon*, Latinised to *dunum* in many places on the continent, meaning an enclosed, safe place or city; and *bach*, meaning small.

DINAS. A fort or camp.

DINAS. The original name was *Pen-dinas*, from the fortified structure on the headland, *pen* or promontory.

DINAS MAWDDWY. From *Dinas*, an enclosed town or fort, and the name of the river. *Mawddwyd* is derived from *Maw*, meaning broad, and *gwy*, meaning many turns. But it could derive from *Maw-dwy*, the goddess Maw.

DINAS POWIS. Probably an indication that a *dinas*, or fort, was built here by a Prince of Powys, the ancient territory which the county of that name now covers. Popular opinion had it that the correct spelling was *Denis*, after the daughter of a Prince of Powys for whom the fortified dwelling place may have been built.

DINGSTOW. The orignal was *Merthyr Dingad*, the burial place of Dingad, a saint. Stow in English means a sacred place.

DOLBADARN. This means the meadow, *dôl*, of St. Padarn. *Dolau* means meandering, so that *dôl* came to mean the fertile land in the river valley formed by its meandering course.

DOLFOR. This is a corruption of *dôl*, meaning meadow, and *fawr*, large or great.

DOLGELLAU. This is a compound of *dôl*, land by a river or meadow, and *gellau*, the plural of *gell* or *cell* – monk's cells.

DOWLAIS. This is probably derived from *clais*, meaning a ditch or stream, and *du*, meaning black. This is most probably the same word as Doulas in Powys, Dowles in Salop and Dawlish in Devon.

DREFELIN. This is a combination of *tref*, meaning homestead, and *melin*, a mill.

DWYRAIN. This is a combination of *dwy*, two, and *rhan*, part or partition. Legend has it that the village was divided into two by Idwal, Prince of Wales, giving one half to St. Beuno and the other to the Bishop of Bangor.

DYFFRYN. This word is derived from *dwfr*, meaning water, and *hynt*, a way or course. In effect, therefore, it means the course of a river, and has come to mean a valley.

DYFFRYN ELAN. *Dyffryn*, the course of the river, or valley. *Elan*, the name of the river which runs through it.

DYFNANT. This is derived from *dwfn*, meaning deep, and *nant*, meaning a stream or riverbed.

DYLIFE. This is almost certainly the word *dylif*, which means a flood, or floods.

DYSERTH. This comes from *diserth*, meaning a wilderness. It is itself derived from the Latin *desertus*, a desert, and indicates that it was the dwelling place of a hermit or religious recluse. In former times it was known as *Castell-y-Ffaidon* and *Castell Ceri*. Dysart in Scotland and Dyzard in Cornwall probably derive from the same word.

EDEYRN. Probably named after Edeyrn ap Nudd, since the church is dedicated to St. Edeirnion.

EFAILNEWYDD. *Efail*, smithy; *newydd*, new.

EGLWYSBACH. *Eglwys*, church; *bach*, small.

EGLWYSWRW. The church of Wrw or Eirw.

EGLWYS Y DRINDOD. *Eglwys*, church; *y Drindod*, of the Trinity.

EITHINOG. Place of gorse.

ELY. The Welsh name is *Trelai*, a homestead on the river *Llai*, which means brown-coloured.

ERWOOD. This may be an anglicised form of *Erw-ŷd*, an acre of corn, or a corruption of *y rhyd*, the ford, since there may have been a crossing place on the river Wye here.

ESGAIRGEILIOG. A compound of *esgair*, a leg or mountain ridge, and *ceiliog*, cockerel.

EWENNY. This name derives from *Aventia*, the name of a Celtic goddess in France.

21

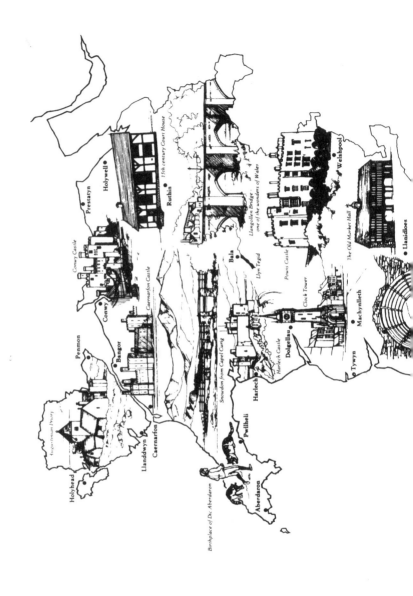

Holyhead

Llanddwyn

Caernarfon

Penmon

Bangor

Conwy

Conwy Castle

Caernarfon Castle

Holyhead (Penmon Priory)

Birthplace of Dic Aberdaron

Aberdaron

Pwllheli

Harlech

Harlech Castle

Snowdon from Capel Curig

Dolgellau

Clock Tower

Tywyn

Machynlleth

Prestatyn

Holywell

Ruthin

15th century Court House

Bala

Llyn Tegid

Llangollen Bridge – one of the wonders of Wales

Powis Castle

Welshpool

The Old Market Hall

Llanidloes

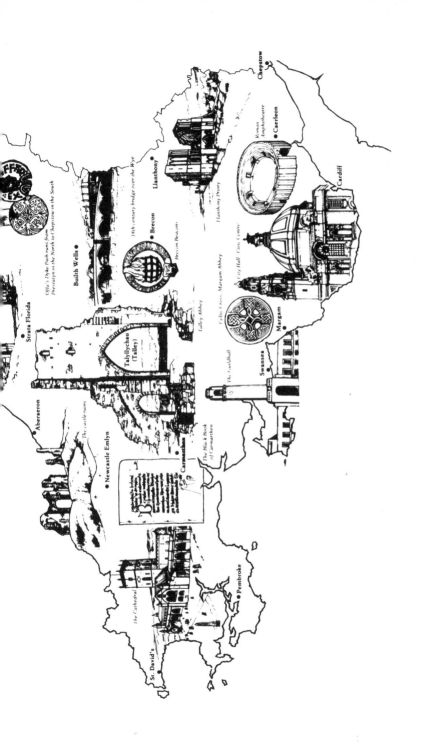

Chepstow

Roman Amphitheatre

Caerleon

Llanthony

Llanthony Priory

Cardiff

18th century bridge over the Wye

Brecon

Ogfa's Dyke Path runs from Prestatyn in the North to Chepstow in the South

Builth Wells

Brecon Beacons

City Hall Civic Centre

Celtic Cross Margam Abbey

Margam

Strata Florida

Talley Abbey

The Guildhall

Swansea

Talyllychau (Talley)

Aberaeron

The castle ruins

Newcastle Emlyn

Carmarthen

The Black Book of Carmarthen

St. David's

The Cathedral

Pembroke

FAWNOG. Place of peat.

FEDW. Birch trees.

FELINDRE. This is probably a compound of *melin* (or *felin*), mill, and *tre*, meaning homestead. Some believe that it may be a corruption of *vileindref*, the villein's home, a villein in mediaeval times being a tenant farmer tied to his lord's land.

FELINFACH. This is *y felin fach*, the small mill.

FELIN NEWYDD. *Melin*, or *y felin*, the mill; *newydd*, new.

FERRYSIDE. This name speaks for itself. Near the mouth of the Towy or Tawe, passengers were ferried over the river to Llanstephan.

FOEL. A bare-topped hill.

FISHGUARD. The Welsh name is *Abergwaun*, the mouth of the river *Gwaun*, which means a moor or meadow. A case of the river taking its name from its surroundings.

FFAIRFACH. This is a compound of *ffair*, a fair, and *bach*, small.

FFESTINIOG. This most probably means Ffestin's land, though many possible derivations have been adduced to it.

FLATHOLM. This was a Danish settlement from around the year 918 A.D. The original word was *fladholmene*, a flat island or grassy bank by water.

FLINT. The name of the town may be taken from the Latinised name of the nearby castle, *Castellum-super-fluentum*, the castle near the sea.

FRON. Hillside.

GAERWEN. A compound of *gaer*, or *caer*, fortifications, and *wen*, the feminine of *gwyn*, meaning white or blessed.

GARNDOLBENMAEN. A combination of *garn*, heap of stones or cairn; *dôl*, meadow; *pen*, head or top, and *maen*, a rock. A cairn at the top of the rock in the meadow.

GARREG. Stone, rock or cliff.

GEIFR. Goats.

GELLIGAER. From *gelli* or *celli*, a common old Welsh name for a grove of trees; *gaer* from *caer*, a fortified place.

24

GILFACH GOCH. *Cilfach,* a small recess or place of retreat; *coch,* red. The latter word may refer to ironworks which used to stand here.

GLAN. Edge of the sea or river; bank.

GLASBURY. The original name may have been *Clas ar Wy,* the cloisters, or religious establishments, on the river Wye. Others derive it from *glas,* meaning green, with the English suffix -bury, borough.

GLYNCEIRIOG. *Glyn,* a glen or deep valley, of the river *Ceiriog,* which means friendly.

GLYN CLYWEDOG. Valley of the Clywedog. *Clywedog* means noisy.

GLYNCORRWG. *Glyn,* a steep-sided valley. *Corrwg* is the stream that runs through it. *Corrwg* probably derives from an obsolete word for brook.

GLYNDYFRDWY. *Glyn* means valley, valley of the river Dyfrdwy. *Dyfr* means water, *dwy* derives from *dwywes,* the old word for goddess. Dover has the same basis.

GLYN NEDD. The valley of the Nedd. Although in modern Welsh *nedd* means nits, applied to the river it most probably means meandering.

GOODWICK. This may be a corruption of the Welsh *coedwig,* a forest, but more likely derives from *good* and *wick,* the Norse for a creek or anchorage.

GORLAN. (Sheep) fold.

GORS. Marsh.

GOWERTON. The Gower peninsula takes its name from the word *gwyr,* which means crooked or warped. It applies to the fact that the peninsula seems to have swerved away from the general coastline, and the shape of its coast which has many inlets and bays.

Gowerton was originally called Gower Road, though the ratepayers of the parish decided to change its name to Gowerton, from January 1, 1886.

GRAIG. Rock or crag.

GRESFORD. A corruption of *groesffordd,* a crossroad.

GRESHOLM. Another testimony to foreign incursions into the southern regions of Wales. Gresholm is compounded of *grass-holm,* a grassy island.

GRUG. Heather.

GWAENYSCOR. Probably a combination of *gwaen,* a meadow; *is,* below or under, and *caer,* a fort.

GWALCHMAI. This is the Welsh name for one of the Knights of the Round Table.

GWERNDDWR. A Combination of *gwyn*, white, and the suffix *-dŵr*, water.

GWIBERNANT. *Gwiber*, viper; *nant*, brook. Viper's brook.

GWBERT. Probably a compound of *gwy-*, signifying water, and *pert*, meaning pretty.

GWYNFE. *Gwyn*, white or fair; *fe*, a mutation of the old Welsh *mai*, a plain. *Gwynfa* or *Gwynfyd* is the Welsh for Paradise.

GWYDDELWERN. Marsh of the Irishman.

HAFAN. Haven. Protecting place.

HAFOD YR YNYS. *Hafod*, summer pasture land; *yr ynys*, on the island.

HAFREN. River Severn.

HALKYN. A corruption of the Welsh word *helygain*, willow trees. The village lies at the base of a mountain of this name.

HARLECH. In ancient times the site of a castle was known as *Tŵr Bronwen*, Bronwen's Tower, after Bronwen of the White Nest, sister of Bran ap Llyr, King of Britain. Her sad story is to be found in the Mabinogion.

After Edward I built his castle there it was called *Hardd-llech*, the beautiful stone or rock.

Tŷ Mawr, Gwibernant - birthplace of Bishop William Morgan

HAVERFORDWEST. The Welsh name is *Hwllffordd*, perhaps derived from *hwyl*, sail, and *ffordd*, a way. It seems likely that small sailing ships were able to make their way up the creek from what is now Pembroke Dock. The English appellation is more confusing, though it may be a corruption of *aber*, mouth of the river, i.e. where it joins the estuary, and *ffordd*, a way, though it might be the English ford. West was probably added to distinguish the town from another Haverford in the vicinity.

HAY ON WYE. The original name was *Gelli Gandryll*. *Gelli* means a grove of trees. *Gandryll* is very interesting. *Candryll* is often used to describe something that has broken into very small pieces. Could it be from *cant*, a hundred, and *dryll*, piece or gun?

HENLLAN. *Hen*, ancient; *llan*, church.

HENLLYS. *Hen*, old or ancient; *llys*, court or hall.

HIRWAUN. *Hir*, long; *waun*, meadow. In former times it was known as *Hirwaun Gwrgant*, Gwrgant's long meadow, which was said to stretch for a distance of ten miles from Blaengwrach to Mountain Ash.

HOLT. This is a Norse word meaning a wood or refuge for wild animals. The ancient name may have been *Castell Lleon*, castle of the legions. If this is true the present name would be taken from a family of this name who held the castle.

HOLYHEAD. The Welsh name is *Caergybi*, the fort of Cybi, or perphaps *côr Cybi*. the choir of Cybi. The 4th century St. Cybi was given refuge by the Prince of Mona (Anglesey). Holyhead may indicate English recognition of the sanctity of Cybi's life, or the number of religious foundations in the area. Some think the correct wording is Holyhead, a direct translation of *pencelyn*.

HOLYWELL. A free translation of *Treffynnon*. Homestead, *tre*, by the well, *ffynnon*. This is the site of the famous St. Winifred's Well, of legendary fame in curing bodily ills. The Gothic building covering the spring is supposed to have been built by Margaret, Countess of Richmond, and mother of Henry VI.

HUBBERSTON. Named in memory of Hubber or Hubba, a Norse warrior, who, with his brother Hingua, led the invasion into Dyfed in 866.

KIDWELLY. Many forms of this ancient name have appeared over the years. It has been suggested that the old Welsh form was *Cadweli*, a tribal name from Cadwal, a personal name.

KNIGHTON. The Welsh name is *Trefyclawdd*. *Tref,* homestead; *y clawdd,* on the embankment. It is situated close to Offa's Dyke. The English name dates from after the Norman conquest of this part of Wales and was included in a knight's estates.

L

LAMPETER. An Anglicised version of *Llanbedr,* the church of St. Peter. The full name is *Llanbedr Pont Steffan,* St. Peter's church of Stephen's bridge.

LAUGHARNE. The name may be an anglicisation of *Tal-llacharn,* the end of the river *Llacharn,* flashing. Other old Welsh names are *Talycoran* or *Abercoran,* the end or mouth of the river Coran which flows into the river Taf.

LAVERNOCK. This is probably a Norman corruption of *Llanwernog* or – *gwaunog,* the church on a meadow.

LETTERSTON. A translation of the Welsh name *Trelettert,* Lettard's home.

LIBANUS. Lebanon.

LLANAELHAEARN. The church of Aelhaiarn, a 6th century saint.

LLANARTH. *Llan,* a church; *garth,* a hill or enclosure.

LLANARTHNEY. The church of Arthen, son of Brychan.

LLANASA. *Llan,* church; *-asa,* is probably an abbreviation of St. Asaph, a 6th century saint.

LLANBABO. The church may have been founded by Pabo Post Prydain, an eminent warrior who, in later life, turned to religion.

LLANBADARN. The church of St. Padarn. St. Padarn was probably a Breton who came to Wales in 516. He established a number of religious foundations in Wales.

LLANBADRIG. The church of St. Patrick. This is the St. Patrick of Irish fame who stayed for a time in Cybi's seminary on Mona.

LLANBEDROG. The church dedicated to its founder, Pedrog, of the 7th century.

LLANBERIS. The church of Peris, who, apparently, was sent on an evangelising mission from Rome, and died here in the 6th century.

LLANBOIDY. *Llan,* church; *boidy,* may be a corruption of *beudy,* a cowshed. Others think the word derives from *Lan-bod-Dewi,* the church in which St. David dwelt.

LLANBRYNMAIR. *Llan,* church; *bryn,* hill; *Mair,* Mary.

28

LLANDDERFEL. Church dedicated to Derfel. This may be Derfel Gadarn, a 6th century warrior.

LLANDDEUSANT. Church dedicated to *dau sant,* two saints.

LLANDDOWROR. The church of the water men, *dyfrwyr,* so called because the monks of this establishment were forbidden to drink anything but water. St. David was one.

LLANDDWYN. Church dedicated to St. Deuwen, Dynwen or Dwynwen, one of the first converts to Christianity. She is celebrated in Wales in the same way as St. Valentine – the patron saint of sweethearts.

LLANDECWYN. Church of Tecwyn, a 6th century saint. His name is to be found in many places in the area.

LLANDEGLA. Church dedicated to Tegla. Tradition asserts that he was converted to Christianity by the Apostle Paul and was martyred by Nero.

LLANDEILO. The church of St. Teilo, who died in 566.

LLANDDEWIBREFI. The church of *Dewi,* St. David, on the river *Brefi,* which means bleating or lowing, i.e. *noisy.*

LLANDINAM. The proper spelling is *Llandinan. Llan,* church; *dinan,* small port or enclosure.

LLANDORE. The correct spelling is *Glandwr – glan,* river bank; *dŵr,* water.

LLANDOVERY. An anglicisation of *Llanymddyfri,* the church among the many waters.

LLANDRILLO. The church of St. Trillo. There are many places in Wales dedicated to this saint.

LLANDRINDOD. Church of the Trinity. Its ancient name may have been *Fynnon Llwyn y Gog,* the well of the cuckoo's grove.

LLANDUDNO. The church of St. Tudno, of the 6th century. A rocking-stone on the Great Orme's Head is known as *Crud Tudno,* Tudno's cradle.

LLANDWROG. The church of St. Twrog.

LLANDYBIE. The church of St. Tybie, a daughter of Brychan, who lived in the 5th century. Legend has it that she was murdered on this spot, where a church was dedicated to her memory.

LLANDYSUL. The church of St. Tysul, a 6th century saint.

LLANDYRNOG. Church dedicated to Dyrnog.

LLANEDWEN. The church is supposed to have been founded by St. Edwen, niece or daughter of the Saxon King Edwin, in the 6th and 7th century.

LLANEILIAN. The church is named after the pilgrim and saint of the very early Christian era, Eilian Geimiad.

LLANELLI. Church dedicated to St. Ellyw, a saint of the 5th century. Its proper name is *Llanelliw*.

LLANERFYL. Church dedicated to Erfyl.

LLANFAELOG. The church was dedicated in about the 7th century to Maelog. Close by is *Llyn Maelog*, Maelog's Lake.

LLANFACHRETH. The church is dedicated to the 7th century St. Machraith, who founded churches all over Gwynedd, including Mona.

LLANFAGLAN. The church of Baglan.

LLANFAIR CAEREINION. *Llanfair*, St. Mary's church; *Caer-Einion*, Einion's fort.

LLANFAIR DYFFRYN CLWYD. *Llanfair*, the church of St. Mary; *dyffryn*, valley, of Clwyd. *Clwyd* means a hurdle.

LLANFAIRFECHAN. The church of St. Mary. The suffix *-fechan* means small and distinguishes the church from a large establishment near Conwy.

LLANFAIR MATHAFARN EITHAF. *Llanfair*, the church of St. Mary; *Mathafarn*, the place of the tavern; *eithaf*, furthest, extreme. The last word distinguishes the place from the adjoining parish.

LLANFAIR P.G. The full name is *Llanfairpwllgwyngyll-gogerychwyrndrobwll-llantysiliogogogoch*. *Llanfair*, the church of St. Mary; *pwll*, pool; *gwyn*, white; *cyll*, hazel wood; *goger y chwyrn drobwyll*, by the churning whirlpool; *llan Tysilio*, St. Tysilio; *ogogoch*, of the red cave.

LLANFAIR TALHAIARN. The church of St. Mary founded by Talhaiarn, a celebrated bard of the 6th century who devoted the latter part of his life to a saintly existence.

LLANFECHELL. Church dedicated to Mechell or Mechyll, a Welsh bishop of the 7the century.

LLANFERRES. The church dedicated to Berres, possibly a disciple of St. Martin.

LLANFIHANGEL Y GREUDDYN. *Llanfihangel*, the church of Michael the Archangel; *y Greuddyn* may be derived from *creu*, blood, and *dun*, a fort.

LLANFYLLIN. Church dedicated to Myllin.

LLANGADFAN. Church dedicated to St. Cadfan. An old manuscript says that 'This Cadvan, being a nobleman and son-in-law of the King of Armorica (Brittany) came over with Uthr Bendragon, or his son King Arthur.' He settled on *Ynys Enlli*, Bardsley Island. Many of his followers dedicated churches to him.

LLANGADOG. The church of St. Cadoc, who was martyred in Brittany in 490.

LLANGAIN. The church of St. Cain.

LLANGAMARCH. Church on the river Cammarch. *Cam*, astride; *march*, horse.

LLANGEFNI. Church on the river Cefni.

LLANGERNYW. The church is said to have been founded by St. Digain in the 5th century, whose father is said to have been the British king Cystenyn Gernev, son of the Prince of Cornwall, *Cernyw*. Hence Llangernyw.

LLANGOED. *Llan*, church; *coed*, of the wood.

LLANGOLLEN. The church of St. Collen, a seventh century saint who once served in the Roman army. He became Abbot of Glastonbury, but spent the latter part of his life in this quiet beautiful valley.

LLANGORS. A contraction of *Llan-yn-y-gors*, the church in the marsh.

LLANGRANNOG. The church of St. Cranog.

LLANGRISTIOLUS. The church of Cristiolus.

LLANGURIG. Church dedicated to St. Curig, who lived in the 7th century.

LLANGWNADL. The original name was *Nant gwnadl*, not deriving from St. Gwynhoedl as is often believed.

LLANGYBI. The church of St. Cybi, a well-known British saint of the 6th century.

LLANGYNHAFAL. Church dedicated to Cynhafal, a 7the century saint.

The ruins of Valle Crucis Abbey, Llangollen

31

LLANGYNDIR. Church of St. Cynidr. He was the grandson of Brychan whose family did a great deal to further the cause of Christianity in Wales.

LLANIADEN. *Llan*, church; *iaden* is a corruption of the Welsh saint's name, Aeddan.

LLANIDLOES. Church of the 7th century, St. Idloes.

LLANIESTYN. The church is dedicated to its founder, Iestyn ap Geraint.

LLANILAR. The church of St. Hilary, a 6th century saint.

LLANILLTYD FAWR. One of the centres of early Christianity, the appellation *fawr* (mawr), great, distinguishes it from other places of this name. It was probably dedicated to Illtyd in the 5th century.

LLANLLECHID. The church of the female saint, Llechid, who lived in the 6th century.

LLANLLWCH. Church of the swamp or lake. In a low situation, given to flooding.

LLANON. Church dedicated to Nonn, the mother of St. David, patron saint of Wales.

LLANOVER. *Llan*, church; over is a corruption of Mimor. The church of St. Mimor.

LLANPUMSAINT. The church of five saints.

LLANRHAEADR-YM-MOCHNANT. *Llan*, church; *rhaeadr*, waterfall; *ym*, the; *moch*, pig; *nant*, brook or valley.

LLANRHYSTUD. The church of Rhystud, who lived in the 6th century.

LLANRUG. An enclosed place where heather grows (*grug* means heather).

LLANRWST. The old church was built in 1170 and dedicated to the 7th century saint, Crwst. This was burned down, and the present building begun in 1470.

LLANSADWRN. Church dedicated to Sadwrn.

LLANSAMLET. Church founded by Samled.

LLANSANNAN. Church dedicated to Senau, an Irish saint and bishop of the 6th century.

LLANSANTFFRAID. The church of St. Ffraid.

LLANTHONY. Its original name was *Nant Hodni*, the valley of the river Hodni, which is the same river which runs through Brecon, its present name being Honddu. *Hon* means blessed, happy; *ddu*, black.

LLANTRISANT. Church of three saints, supposedly Illtyd, Tyfodwg and Gwynno.

LLANUWCHLLYN. The church above the lake *-llyn.* It is situated near Llyn Tegid.

LLANWRDA. The church may have been dedicated to St. Cawdraf. Other derivations are the church of y *gŵr-da,* the holy man; or *gŵr-daf,* the man of the Taf. This word refers to St. Teilo, who lived for a while by the river.

LLANWRIN. The church of Gwrhin.

LLANWRTYD. Probably a church dedicated to St. Wrtyd. Others believe that the word is a contraction of *Llan-wrth-y-rhyd,* the church by the ford.

LLANYSTUMDWY. Here the two rivers Dwyfor and Dwyfach meet. *Dwy* was an old word for goddess of a river. The large and the small rivers. *Ystum* means a bend in the river.

LLANYWERN. A compound of *Llan,* church; *y gwern or gwernen,* of the alder trees.

LLECHRYD. A compound of *llech,* a flat stone, and *rhyd,* a ford. The ford over the flat stone.

LLITHAFAEN. *Llith* implies attraction and mean means stone. Some sources say there is a loadstone, magnetic stone, in the vicinity.

LLOC. The word means a shelter or dam. In this case it may well imply a sheepfold.

LLWYNGWRIL. Gwril's grove.

LLYN. Lake or pool.

LLYS. Court or mansion.

MACHYNLLETH. The plain or lowlands of Cynllaith.

MAENCLOCHOG. *Maen,* a stone; *clochog,* bell like.

MAENTWROG. *Maen,* rock, of Twrog, a saint of the 15th century.

MAERDY. *Maer* means a steward or local official. *Maerdy* is the steward's house.

MAESTEG. *Maes,* a field; *-teg,* fair.

MALLDRAETH. *Mall* means corrupt, though it may denote wetness; *traeth* iş a beach.

MALLWYD. *Ma* means lowland or field; *llwyd* means grey. The grey field.

MANOBIER. This is probably a corruption of *maenor-Pyr* – Pyr's manor.

MARCHWIAIL. *March* means a horse, a stallion, and the word is used to signify a coarse thing, as in English e.g. horse-chestnut, horse-radish. *Gwiail* means rods-coarse rods.

MARGAM. Most probably a corruption of the personal name Morgan.

MEIFOD. A combination of *mei*, implying mid-way, and *bod*, dwelling. The English equivalent would probably be 'half-way house'. It would be a place where strangers would be put to stay overnight.

MENAI BRIDGE. The Welsh name is *Porthaethwy*. *Porth*, port; *aeth*, terrible; *wy*, water. Menai is derived from *main-wy*, the narrow water.

MERTHYR TYDFIL. The word *Merthyr* is usually followed by the name of a saint and it signifies where that saint was buried. In this case Tudful was the daughter of Brychan, and she was murdered by the pagan Saxons, together with her husband and father.

MILFORD HAVEN. The Welsh name is *Aber-dau-gleddau*. Two streams meet near here, the Cleddau Fawr and Cleddau Fach, greater and lesser swords. Hence the name, the mouth of the two swords.

MOCHDRE. *Moch*, pigs: *-dre* from *tref*, homestead.

MOELFRE. *Moel*, bare; *fre* from *bre*, a hill.

MOLD. The Welsh name is *Yr Wyddgrug*, deriving from *Wytgruc*. *Wyt* is a shortened form of *gŵydd*, a burial mound. The burial mound of Gruc. The English name is a relic of the Norman invasion.

MORFA BYCHAN. Near Porthmadog popular caravan centre, next to Black Rock Sands. *Morfa* means bog or sea-marsh; *bychan* is little.

MORRISTON. Named after Sir John Morris, who built a copper works here in 1876, round which the town grew.

MOSTYN. Probably a corruption of *maes*, meadow, and *din*, fortress. Apparently the first person to adopt this as a personal name was Thomas ap Richard ap Hywel ap Ithel Fychan.

MYDDFAI. *Mydd* means a large pan. *Fai* means of the plain or field.

MYNYTHO. A corruption of *mynyddoedd*, mountains.

NANNERCH. A combination of *nant*, stream, and *erch*, coloured.

NANTCWNLLE. *Nant*, stream; *cwnlle* is probably a corruption of Cunllo, a saint of the 5th century.

NANTFFRANCON. *Nant,* stream or small valley; *ffrancon,* a word applied before the Norman invasion to a mercenary soldier; it probably applies to the Germanic forces which infiltrated parts of Wales.

NANTGAREDIG. *Nant,* a stream; *caredig* means kindly, though in this case it may be a proper name, Caredig's brook.

NANTGARW. *Nant,* stream or small valley; *garw,* rough or rugged.

NANTGLAS. Blue or green stream.

NANTMEL. Either Mael's brook or *nant,* brook; *mêl,* honey, honeybook.

NANTYFFIN. *Nant,* stream; *ffin,* boundary. Natural divisions such as streams and ditches often mark county or parish boundaries.

NANTYGLO. *Nant* valley or stream; *y-glo,* of the coal.

NARBERTH. In the Mabinogion this is called *Arberth,* a place among the bushes or hedges. It was probably preceded by the preposition *yn,* hence Narberth.

NEATH. The name of the river is Nedd, from which the town takes its name. Nedd itself may derive from the Latin *nidum.*

NEFYN. The church here was probably dedicated to Nefyn, daughter of Brychan and a saint of the 5th century.

NEUADD. Hall or mansion.

NEWBOROUGH. Its ancient name was probably *Rhos-hir,* long moorland. Once the capital of Mona, it was the residence of the princes of North Wales. Under Edward I the township was made a free corporation and the present name dates from this time. Its Welsh translation is *Niwbwrch.*

NEWCASTLE EMLYN. The Welsh name is *Castell-newydd-Emlyn,* new castle in the territory of Emlyn. The castle is built on the site of a much older construction by Sir Rhys ap Thomas in the reign of Henry VIII.

NEWPORT. The Welsh name is *Trefdraeth. Tref,* homestead or town; *draeth,* beach.

NEYLAND. This is a Norman appellation from eyland, island, with the prefix *n.* Nayland in Suffolk and Nyland in Somerset have the same derivation.

NORTHOP. A Saxon name, North-thorpe, Northtown.

O

OGOF. Cave.

OXWICH. Ox is derived from the Welsh *wysg,* current, water (from which we have Usk, Esk, Exe); -wich is probably derived from the Norse -*wic,* a creek.

OYSTERMOUTH. This is corruption of the Welsh name *Ystumllwynarth. Ystum* means a bend in a river or cliff. *Llwynarth* is a bear's grove. Or *arth* could be a corruption of *garth,* a hill or military encampment.

P

PAINSCASTLE. A castle was built by the Norman family of de Pain. Their name is also preserved in Paignton, Devon.

PANDY. *Pandy* means a fulling mill.

PANTYCELYN. *Pant,* hollow, *y celyn,* of the holly trees.

PEMBROKE DOCK. Originally a small village called Pater or Paterchurch; it was called Pembroke Dock in 1814.

PENARTH. This means headland, or head of the promontory.

PENCADER. *Pen.* head; *cader,* seat or fortress.

PENCLAWDD. *Pen,* head; *clawdd,* embankment, often a military fortification.

PENDERYN. This may be a corruption of *Penydaren,* the end of a rocky outcrop.

PENDINE. *Pen,* head or end; *tywyn,* sand-dunes.

PENMACHNO. Head of the river Machno. *Machno* may mean swift.

PENMAENMAWR. *Pen,* head; *maen,* rock; *mawr,* great.

PENNANT MELANGELL. *Pen-nant,* head of the stream. Melangell is a personal name.

PENRHYNDEUDRAETH. *Penrhyn,* headland; *deu,* two; *traeth,* beach.

PENTRAETH. *Pen,* head; *traeth,* beach.

PENTREBERW. Berw village. *Berw* might mean watercress.

PENTREFOELAS. *Pentre,* village; *moel,* bare hilltop; *glas,* green. Village of the green hill.

PISTYLL. Spout, conduit; fall, cataract.

PLAS. A mansion.

PONTARDAWE. Bridge over the *Tawe*, the still and silent water.

PONTARDDULAIS. Bridge over the river *Dulais*, black water.

PONTARFYNACH (DEVIL'S BIDGE). The bridge over the river *Mynach*, which means monk, perhaps one of the monks of nearby Strata Florida Abbey. Called Devil's Bridge after the legend that it was constructed by Satan in order to gain the soul of an old woman. He did not succeed.

PONTARGOTHI. Bridge over the river Cothi.

PONTERWYD. Bridge of poles, or bridge with a handrail.

PONTNEDDFECHAN. *Pont*, bridge, of the lesser river Nedd.

PONTRHYDFENDIGAID. Originally *Rhyd-bendigaid*, ford of the blessed ones. Probably the monks of Strata Florida. The *pont*, bridge, was added later.

PONTRHYDYGROES. *Pont*, bridge; *rhyd*, ford; *y groes*, of the cross.

PONTISCYLL. *Pont*, bridge *sticyll* derived from *ystigl*, a stile. Apparently there used to be an old bridge here with a stile at either end.

PONTYATES. *Pont-iets*, bridge of the gates. There were toll-gates nearby.

PONTYBEREM. Bridge over the river Berem. *Berem* may be derived from *berw*, boiling.

PONTYPRIDD. Bridge by the earthen house, *pidd*, meaning wattle and daub.

PORTHCAWL. Harbour of the Gauls, possibly harbour of the sea-cabbage.

PORTHMADOG. Harbour of Madog or Maddocks. W.A. Maddocks constructed the embankment called the Cob, reclaiming 7,000 acres of land.

PORT TALBOT. The name was changed from Aberafon Harbour by Act of Parliament in 1836. Talbot is a family name.

PRESCELLY. The Welsh form is *Preseli*. *Pres* comes from *prys*, a grove. *Selev* is the Welsh form for Solomon.

PRESTATYN. This may be a corruption of *Prysgoed-ddin; prys*, brushwood; *coed*, wood; *din*, fortress.

PRESTEIGN. The Welsh name is *Llanandras*, the church of St. Andrew. The English word means priest's town, the same derivation as Preston.

PUNCHESTON. The Welsh name is *Casmael*, probably a contraction of *Castell Maelgwyn*, Maelgwyn's Castle. Puncheston may derive from the Flemish name Poyntz.

PWLLHELI. *Pwll*, pool; *heli*, salt-water.

R

REYNOLDSTON. Reynold's town. Reynold was probably one of the Flemish settlers who came here in the reign of Henry I.

RHANDIRMWYN. *Rhandir*, land, probably hereditary. According to the old laws, there were four *tyddyns* or smallholdings. *Mwyn* could be a pleasant place, or could refer to minerals.

RHAYADR. The word means a waterfall.

RHIW. The name means a hillside.

RHONDDA. This may be derived from *Rhoddneu*, babbling stream, or possibly *Yr Honddu*, the black (river).

RHOSLLANNERCHRUGOG. *Rhos*, moorland; *llannerch*, a small enclosure; *crugog*, heaps of stones. Moorland dotted with cairns.

RHOSTRYFAN. *Rhos* means high land or moorland. *Tryfan* means similar to a finger, with a rounded head.

RHOSNEIGR. *Rhos*, moorland; *neigr*, probably black.

RHOSSILI. Possibly from *rhos*, moorland; *heli*, salt-water or sea. It may mean Sulien's moor.

RHOSYBOL. *Rhos* is a marsh. *Bol* means belly, or originally a bag. The name therefore means a large marsh which swallows everything.

RHUDDLAN. Probably a corruption of *Rhyd-y-llan*, the ford by the church. Near here the battle of *Morfa Rhuddlan*, Rhuddlan marsh, was fought between the Saxons under Offa and the Welsh under Caradog in 795. Many place names nearby commemorate this event.

RHYDGWILYM. Gwilym's ford; *Gwilym* is the equivalent of William. Perhaps named after the Rev. William Jones, first Baptist minster of the place.

RHYDYCLAFDY. *Rhyd*, ford; *y clafdy*, by the hospital.

RHYL. The derivation is obscure but may be derived from *yr hel*, the hunting ground, from *hela*, to hunt.

ROWAN. This may be a corruption of *yr-wy-wen*, the white water or river. It is more probably *Y Ro wen*, a place where white grit was quarried.

RUABON. A corruption of *Rhiw Fabon*, hillside of Mabon, a Welsh saint.

RUTHIN. Probably a corruption of *rhudd*, red, and *din*, town. So called from the colour of the soil.

S

ST. ASAPH. The Welsh form is *Llanelwy*, meaning the church by the river Elwy. The name *Elwy* derives from the old Welsh *-gwy*, meaning bends or turns, and *el-* meaning many. Therefore the river with many bends. The English name is an honour of St. Asaph, who was the second Bishop of the see in 560 A.D.

ST. ATHAN. A church was built here by St. Tathan in the 6th century. Legend has it that he founded a monastery here also.

ST. CLEARS. This was one of the early Norman foundations. The church was dedicated to St. Clâr or Clare, who was martyred in Normandy in 894.

ST. DAVID'S. The Welsh name is *Tyddewi*, David's house. St. David is the patron saint of Wales and probably the first to organise systematically the conversion of the Welsh people. He was the grandson of Caredig, who gave his name to a large area of Wales, Ceredigion.

ST. DONAT'S. Donat is an Anglicised form of *Dunawd*, to whom the church was dedicated.

ST. FAGAN'S. St. Fagan is said to have arrived in Britain on an evengelising mission in the year 180 A.D.

ST. NICHOLAS. This was once called Monktown, after its church was granted in 1088 to the Abbey of St. Seyes in Normandy. Shortly afterwards a Priory of Benedictine monks was established dedicated to St. Nicholas.

SARN. *Sarn* means a road. Several roads meet here.

SAUNDERSFOOT. The first part is a contraction of the name Alexander; it means Alexander's place at the foot of the hill.

SKERRIES. The Welsh name is *Ynys y Moelrhoniaid.* The English name comes from the Norwegian *sker*, meaning a pinnacle of rock on land or at sea.

SKOKHOLM. A Norse word meaning wooded land.

SOLVA. The derivation of this name is obscure. It may derive from *sol*, *swl*, meaning muddy, and the suffix *-ach*, water.

STAYLITTLE. The Welsh name is *Penfforddlas*, the end of the green road. The English name comes from a public house of that name.

STRATA FLORIDA. From the Latin *strata*, paved road; *florida*, abounding with flowers. The abbey was founded by Rhys ap Gruffydd and built c. 1184. It is supposed to be the resting place of several Welsh princes.

SWANSEA. The original name was apparently *Cae Wyr*, the fortress of Gower. The present Welsh name is *Abertawe*, from its situation on the estuary of the Tawe river. *Tawe* comes from *tawel*, silent, and *gwy*, the silent water. The English name may commemorate the Dane Sweyn, whose fleet was destroyed by a storm in Swansea bay around 877.

SYCHNANT. Dry stream.

TALACHDDU. *Tal*, end, of the river *Achddu*, black stream, perhaps from its source in the Black Mountain.

TALGARTH. *Tal*, termination; *garth*, jutting hill.

TALYBONT. Bridgend. *Tal*, end; *y -pont*, of the bridge.

TALYLLYCHAU. *Tal*, end; *y-llychau*, of the waters or pools, although a tenth century manuscript explained *lichou* (the old form of llychau) as marshes, not pools or lakes.

TALYLLYN. *Tal*, end, *y-llyn*, of the lake.

TALYSARN. *Tal*, end; *y sarn*, of the road. Probably the Roman road often known as *Sarn Helen*, a Welsh Princess and wife of the famous *Macsen Wledig*, Maximus, who aspired to be Emperor of the Western Roman Empire.

TANYBWLCH. *Tan*, below; *y bwlch*, the pass.

TEMPLETON. Possibly named after the medieval Knights Templar.

TENBY. Dinbych. Small fort.

TIR. Land.

TONYPANDY. *Ton*, a marsh; *pandy*, a black hollow. The marsh of the black hollow.

TONYREFAIL. *Yr efail*, of the smithy. *Ton* here means the skin on the surface of water, probably a marsh.

TOWYN. Place of sand. Beach.

TRAETHCOCH. *Traeth*, beach, sands; *coch*, red.

TRAWSFYNYDD. *Traws*, across; *y mynydd*, the mountain.

TRE. Home, Homestead, Hamlet, Town.

TREDEGAR. The proper spelling is probably *Tredegyr*, the home of Tegyr.

TREFECCA. *Tre*, home of *Becca*. This might be the name of heiress Rebecca Prosser who built her home here in the reign of Elizabeth I.

TREFEGLWYS. *Tref,* hamlet or town; *eglwys,* church.

TREFNANT. A compound of *Tref,* homestead; and *nant,* stream.

TREFOR. *Tre,* home or town; *-for* from *fawr,* large.

TREFRIW. *Tre,* town or homestead; *rhiw,* hill. Town on the hill.

TREGARON. The home of Caron. This town was possbily named after a bishop.

TRELECH. *Tre,* home or town; *llech,* stone.

TREMADOG. *Tre,* town or home; of Madog; possibly Maddocks (see Porthmadog).

TRIMSARAN. A corruption of *trum-sarn,* ridgeway.

TUDWEILIOG. Probably named after St. Tudwal.

TUMBLE. Named after the Tumble Inn. That in turn may be a reference to Cromwell's son Richard, whose nickname was 'Tumble Down Dick'. Wales was largely a centre of Royalist sympathy.

TŶ GWYN. White house.

TYLWCH. *Tŷ,* house; *llwch,* pool or mud.

TYN (TYDDYN). Small farm or cottage.

TYWYN. This is derived from *tywodyn,* sand; place of sand.

USK. The Welsh name is *Wysg* from the Celtic *peisg,* meaning fish, a river full of fish. The word became corrupted to *Wysg,* as the English Usk in turn is a corruption of *Wysg.*

UWCH Y GARREG. Above the rock.

VALLEY. This seems to be a mutilated anglicisation of *mael-dy,* house of profit or trade.

VAN (Fan). A peak.

VELINDRE. Place of the mill.

WAENFAWR. *Waen* from *waun* or *gwaun*, meadow; *fawr*, great.

WELSHPOOL. The Welsh name is *Trallwng*, a marshy place. Probably a reference to the lake below Powis Castle. Probably called Welshpool as a distinction from Poole in Dorset.

WEN (Gwen). White; pure.

WENVOE. The original spelling was *gwynfa*, white or blessed place.

WERNOG. Marshy place.

WHITLAND. This may be a reference to *Hen dŷ Gwyn ar Daf*, the old white house on the Taf, supposedly the residence of *Hywel Dda*, Howel the Good. It may be where he and his advisers revised the old Welsh laws in 927; the Laws of Hywel Dda are renowned for their fairness.

WREXHAM. Probably a compound of *rex* and *ham*, the king's hamlet or village. It may, however, be derived from Wright's ham, Wright's village.

Y. The (before consonants).

YNYS ENLLI. *Ynys*, the island, of Benlli the Giant. Its English name is Bardsey Island as it was used as a refuge by bards or druids in times of persecution. It is also known as the Isle of 20,000 Saints.

YSBYTY IFAN. *Ysbyty*, hospice or hospital of Ifan; supposedly founded by Ifan ab Rhys in 1189.

YSGUBOR. Barn.

YSTALYFERA. From *ynys*, which generally means an island, but also, as here, flat land by a river, or water. It often happens that *ynys* is reduced to *ys*, or just *-s-* in a place name. *Tal* means above and *y fera* comes from *bera*, a sheaf of hay or corn. The mountain behind the village is called *Y Fera*.

YSTRAD. Valley, Dale, Flat. A river in Denbigh.

YSTRADFELLTE. *Ystad* means a flat piece of land, the bottom of a river valley. *Mellte* is the name of the river, which means swift as lightening.

YSTRADGYNLAIS. The valley of the river Cynlais.

YSTRAD MYNACH. *Ystrad*, valley; *mynach*, monk. The correct wording might be *Ystrad Maenarch*, after Maenarch, one-time Earl of Hereford.